ZEBRAS

by JoAnn Early Macken

Reading consultant: Susan Nations, M.Ed., author/literacy coach/consultant

WEEKLY (WR) READER®
EARLY LEARNING LIBRARY

Please visit our web site at: www.earlyliteracy.cc
For a free color catalog describing Weekly Reader® Early Learning Library's
list of high-quality books, call 1-877-445-5824 (USA) or 1-800-387-3178 (Canada).
Weekly Reader® Early Learning Library's fax: (414) 336-0164.

Library of Congress Cataloging-in-Publication Data

Macken, JoAnn Early, 1953-
    Zebras / by JoAnn Early Macken.
       p. cm. — (Animals I see at the zoo)
    Summary: Photographs and simple text introduce the physical characteristics
and behavior of zebras, one of many animals kept in zoos.
    Includes bibliographical references and index.
    ISBN 0-8368-3277-9 (lib. bdg.)
    ISBN 0-8368-3290-6 (softcover)
    1. Zebras—Juvenile literature. 2. Zoo animals—Juvenile literature. [1. Zebras.
2. Zoo animals.] I. Title.
QL737.U62M32   2002
590.66'7 Jc2i   2002016868

This edition first published in 2002 by
Weekly Reader® Early Learning Library
330 West Olive Street, Suite 100
Milwaukee, WI 53212 USA

Copyright © 2002 by Weekly Reader® Early Learning Library

Art direction: Tammy Gruenewald
Production: Susan Ashley
Photo research: Diane Laska-Swanke
Graphic design: Katherine A. Goedheer

Photo credits: Cover, title, pp. 5, 15 © James P. Rowan; p. 7 © John Gerlach/Visuals
Unlimited; p. 9 © Cheryl A. Ertelt/Visuals Unlimited; pp. 11, 17 © Joe McDonald/Visuals
Unlimited; pp. 13, 19 © Gil Lopez-Espina/Visuals Unlimited; p. 21 © William Muñoz

Printed in the United States of America

1 2 3 4 5 6 7 8 9 06 05 04 03 02

Note to Educators and Parents

Reading is such an exciting adventure for young children! They are beginning to integrate their oral language skills with written language. To encourage children along the path to early literacy, books must be colorful, engaging, and interesting; they should invite the young reader to explore both the print and the pictures.

Animals I See at the Zoo is a new series designed to help children read about twelve fascinating animals. In each book, young readers will learn interesting facts about the featured animal.

Each book is specially designed to support the young reader in the reading process. The familiar topics are appealing to young children and invite them to read — and re-read — again and again. The full-color photographs and enhanced text further support the student during the reading process.

In addition to serving as wonderful picture books in schools, libraries, homes, and other places where children learn to love reading, these books are specifically intended to be read within an instructional guided reading group. This small group setting allows beginning readers to work with a fluent adult model as they make meaning from the text. After children develop fluency with the text and content, the book can be read independently. Children and adults alike will find these books supportive, engaging, and fun!

— Susan Nations, M.Ed., author, literacy coach,
and consultant in literacy development

I like to go to the zoo. I see zebras at the zoo.

All zebras have light skin. All zebras have dark stripes.

Some stripes
are wide.
Some stripes
are narrow.

A zebra's **mane** has stripes. The hair in its mane stands up straight.

mane

Zebras live near water. Some live on mountains. Some live on flat land with few trees.

Zebras eat grass, roots, leaves, and twigs.

A group of zebras is called a **herd**. Zebras stay in a herd to be safe. They all watch for danger.

Look at those
stripes! It is
hard to pick
out one zebra.

I like to see
zebras at the
zoo. Do you?

Glossary

herd — a number of animals feeding or living together

mane — long hair on an animal's neck

narrow — thin, slender

For More Information

Books

Burnie, David. *Mammals. Eyewitness Explorers* (series). New York: Dorling Kindersley, 1998.

Lepthien, Emilie U. *Zebras. New True Book* (series). Chicago: Children's Press, 1994.

Macken, JoAnn Early. *African Animals. Animal Worlds* (series). Milwaukee: Gareth Stevens, 2002.

Shahan, Sherry. *Feeding Time at the Zoo*. New York: Random House, 2000.

Web Sites

Chaffee Zoo

www.chaffeezoo.org/zoo/animals/zebra.html

For a zebra photo and facts

Canadian Museum of Nature

www.nature.ca/notebooks/english/zebra.htm

For a zebra illustration and facts

Index

About the Author

JoAnn Early Macken is the author of a rhyming picture book, *Cats on Judy*, and *Animal Worlds*, a series of nonfiction picture books about animals and their habitats. Her poems have been published or accepted by *Ladybug*, *Spider*, *Highlights for Children*, and an anthology, *Stories from Where We Live: The Great Lakes*. A winner of the Barbara Juster Esbensen 2000 Poetry Teaching Award, she teaches poetry writing. She lives in Wisconsin with her husband and their two sons.